EMOTIONS OF A SUPER SIBLING

TAMARA CULLERE
ILLUSTRATED BY HALEY MCDEVITT

Copyright © 2021 Tamara Cullere

All rights reserved.

No part of this publication in print or in electronic format may be reproduced, stored in a retrieval system, or transmitted in any form or by any means, electronic, mechanical, photocopying, recording, or otherwise without the prior written permission of the publisher.

This is a work of fiction. Names, characters, organizations, places, events and incidents are either the products of the author's imagination or are used fictitiously. Any resemblance to actual persons, living or dead, or actual events is purely coincidental.

Illustrations by Haley McDevitt
Distribution by Bublish, Inc.

ISBN: 978-1-64704-408-4 (paperback)

Tyler and Lucas,
Being a Super sibling is not an easy role to have but every day you amaze me with how you work through the hard parts and find joy.

Benji,
You're not alone on this journey especially with your amazing brothers by your side.

You boys are my world.

"Super Sibling" is a title that I have earned.
Living with my brother leaves me quite concerned.

My older brother has a rare disease.
Hurler's Syndrome is now our area of expertise.

Although I do not have the same medical complications,
I live with the consequences of his limitations.

It is not easy having a brother who is different in many ways.
Learning to cope means that there are different emotions I express on any given day.

Some days, I am PROUD I can help my brother out.
I like being the one to teach him new things
and make him laugh instead of pout.

Other days, I am FRUSTRATED because I don't want to be his helper boy. I want to play and do things with my friends that I enjoy.

Other days, I am ANNOYED at the things
he still hasn't learned how to do.
I want him to run, climb, jump, and play like me, too.

Some days, I am more UNDERSTANDING that he has many different needs. I want to help my parents and watch him succeed.

Other days, I am JEALOUS that he doesn't have to do things alone. I want to be noticed and get extra help, and on those days, I make it very known.

Some days, I am HAPPY that when it comes to him, so many people care. If he ever needs anything, someone will always be there.

Other days, I feel LOST when he gets so much attention. Watching everyone fuss over him and not me causes me so much tension.

Some days, I stay CALM when he is acting out, being mad, or being mean. I know he is feeling frustrated and just wants to be heard and to be seen.

Other days, I get ANGRY right back.
Rather than telling him that he hurt me, I go on the attack.

Some days, I find ADVENTURE in all his special tools and medical supplies. We can pretend he is a villain and that his oxygen tank is part of his disguise.

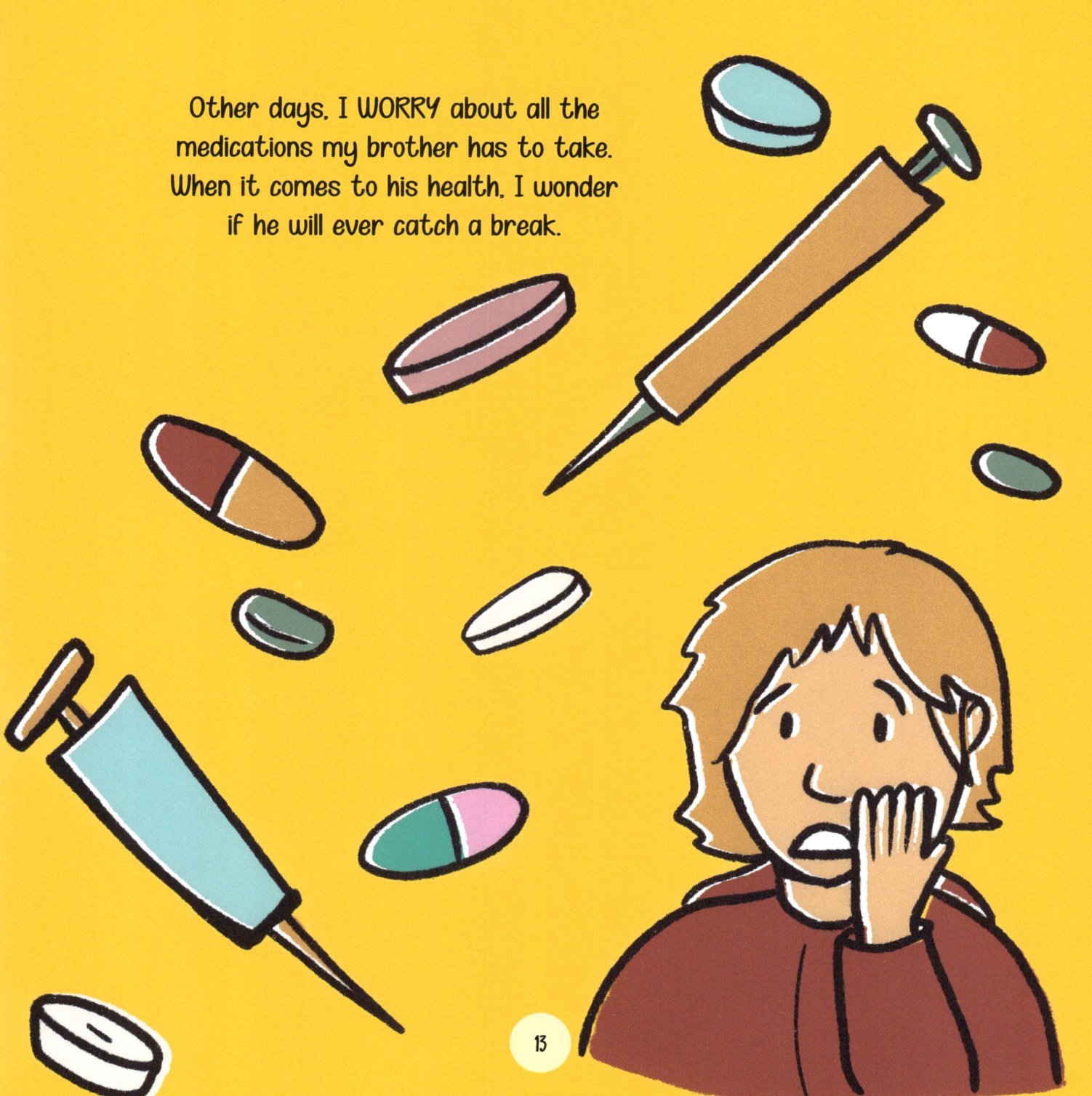
Other days, I WORRY about all the medications my brother has to take. When it comes to his health, I wonder if he will ever catch a break.

Some days, I ENJOY when my brother goes to the doctor for a longer stay. I get special time with my grandparents and get to do things in a different way.

Other days, I have a lot of FEAR when he is in pain or gets sick. I never know if it is serious— if he will end up in the hospital for days or get better quick.

Other days, I get ANXIOUS when I think about how he will be treated.
I don't want new people to make fun of him or, because he is different, make him feel defeated.

Some days, I get so much JOY out of playing and spending time with him. We do many fun things—reading, wrestling, playing pretend, and climbing on our jungle gym.

Other days, I am CONFUSED as to which of us is the older brother. Given his needs, I have learned to take care of him almost as well as my mother.

Some days, I am EXCITED and can't wait to grow older with my brother. I think of all the different experiences and adventures we will eventually have with one another.

Other days, I am SCARED that by the time that I am grown, something bad will have happened to him and I will be left on my own.

Some days, I feel like I have to hide my emotions and fears behind a mask. Being a Super Sibling is rewarding, but it's rarely an easy task.

No matter what Super Siblings say or do, beneath the different emotions, the love for our sibling ALWAYS shines through.

Author's Note

This story was inspired and informed by the real journey my boys have with their brother's diagnosis of Hurler's Syndrome (MPS1). Our oldest son was diagnosed with Hurler's Syndrome at 16-months-old, after a kind stranger recognized some of the facial characteristics and brought it to our attention.

Hurler's Syndrome is a lysosomal storage disease where the body is missing a specific enzyme. The missing enzyme helps break down materials within the cells, and without this material broken down, a buildup occurs that leads to progressive damage of all the body's cells. This causes issues throughout the body, especially in the bones and key organs—like the brain, the eyes, and the heart. Unfortunately, there is no cure, and MPS is a terminal disease.

Currently there are two treatment options available that prolong life expectancy. These include enzyme replacement therapy (ERT) and a stem cell transplant. Neither are easy paths for the child nor the family. Our son had a stem cell transplant at 18-months-old with donated cord blood.

Our life revolves around what our immune suppressed son can and cannot do. We feel blessed to have most of our child's specialists at the Children's

Hospital of Philadelphia (CHOP) where we are able to coordinate care so that departments work together to improve his health and quality of life. We are forever grateful for the care we receive there. With Hurler's Syndrome, our son travels to CHOP one to four times a month for appointments, procedures, and/or even surgery. Doctor's appointments, daily medications, and hospital stays are a normal part of life for our oldest son and his super siblings.

Our youngest two boys have had to learn how to cope with the extra time and attention their older brother gets and come to terms with some of his limitations. This is an ever evolving, yet normal process for them. Despite our oldest child being the only one diagnosed with Hurler's Syndrome, everyone in our family is affected by it in one way or another. This book was written to help validate our sons' experiences or, more generally, the experiences of any sibling of a child who needs a little extra help and support.

For more information on Hurler's Syndrome, please check out https://mpssociety.org/. For more information about the Children's Hospital of Philadelphia and the great specialists there, visit https://www.chop.edu/.